My
Quintessence

Jasmine Farrell

ISBN-13: 9780692280249

To the late Annie and Hugh York.
The greatest *Somebodies* I have met

Foreword:

A plethora of things have changed since I initially published *My Quintessence* in 2014. Since then, I have de-converted from Christianity and have begun the journey of re-discovering myself. I addressed the cognitive dissonance, self-loathing and scriptures that told me that the way I was born didn't line up with God's standards. I chose authenticity over structured religion and the holy book that came along with it. To those who are a part of the Christian faith, I respect your right to live for Christ and hopefully these poems will inspire you. However, I can no longer limit the way I live, love and evolve based on a dogmatic faith. Although, I no longer view life the way that it's conveyed in the following poems, I refuse to cease its publication. I will remember where I've come from and allow readers to witness my growth as well. Cheers to realness!

My Quintessence

ACKNOWLEDGMENTS

I am indebted to my parents for simply believing in me. I adore your strength, Ma. Your perseverance has trickled onto me. My father's support has always made me stable. The prayers, wise words and advice you two relinquished, are the reason why I decided to let people read my core.

Words cannot express how thankful I am for Keneil Buchanan and Andrea Gonzalez-Wheeler. Andrea, you demolished my grammatical errors like a warrior princess! *Thanks, Ms. Lady Editor.* Ken, you supported me like a *Jansport* knapsack (as Ms. Kimberly Jones would put it). From reading every poem I sent you two, to pushing me to keep going despite what I was feeling, I appreciate the two of you. Discouragement would creep into my mind every now and then, but the both of you made sure to hand it an eviction notice.

To the pre-readers: Nichole, Diane Pope, Keturah Harper, Olivia Washington, Shaquaza Dumas and Kwame; I am grateful for your honesty and feedback. I was confident to send you all the manuscript knowing I would get feedback, instead of flattery. A church mother once told me,

"Better to have sour truth than honey lies."

Table of Content

The Introduction

I'm awesomely awkward
and
ridiculously random.
My weirdness cannot be shoved in boxes.
I'm more than a shy girl with her hands in her pockets.
Darn it, I own unicorns!
Born in the village.
Maybe that's why I'm so goofy.
I know my past wounds have given life more beauty.
Maybe that's why my poetry has more potency.
My imagination can burst through stars while eating marshmallows.
Yes, I just personified my imagination.
HELLO!
Honey, I have a glow.
You can't see it,
it's not for show.
Just my essence humming that I'm more than some
average Joe.
I'm Queen of the kinks.
I used to be a part of the voiceless tribe,
until God inscribed me with purpose.
I no longer feel worthless; no longer
a believer in my own pessimism.
Darn it, I'm driven!
Far from coy when stating my boundaries.
I can be transparent like a diary
and guarded like Sloman Shields.
But I always yield to growth.
Got a mind that mumbles meticulously
and a heart that loves ferociously.
Fragile like white lilies, but I'm firm;
I'm stern when I need to be.

Rarely butter up my words or look for honey.
I'm awesomely awkward
and
ridiculously random.
My weirdness cannot be shoved in boxes.
I'm more than a shy girl with her hands in her pockets.
Darn it,
I
own
unicorns.

Get to Know Me

I'm an anthology of paradoxes;
don't you dare put me in a box.
Don't sly your way into my corner
like Fantastic Mr. Fox.
I'll respectfully cross your lines
and prove your irrational generalizations
to be nothing more than fear and ignorance.
I am innocence with flawed stories.
I'm Jasmine.
Get to know me.

Analyzing me will get your feelings hurt, by your
own thoughts.
Placing me on a pedestal will break your own heart.
Being afraid of the truth will make you hate me.
I don't tolerate foolishness so don't degrade me.
Don't make assumptions without knowing my journey.
Drink water when you're thirsty;
eat food when you're hungry.
Be around me if you need something lovely.
I'm Jasmine.
Get to know me.

I'm sweet like Darrell Lea licorice but, firm like an oak tree
So, don't you dare approach me sinisterly
hoping, to use me like a rug.

Honey, this ain't Shaw Floors.
I abhor the preconceived notions
to be used by people who concoct delicious
potions to manipulate.

If I've obtained a nasty habit,
I'll drop it.
I'm a messy perfection whose
attracted to progression.
Don't try to learn me, I'm not a lesson.
I'm an anthology of paradoxes
so, don't you dare put me in a box.
I'll embrace you if, you let me.
Embrace me and I promise
you'll never forget me
I'm Jasmine.
Get to know me.

Have Layers, Lovely

I'm still fighting compromise.
Trying not to prostitute my lines.
I don't want my core to be redefined
into what you struggle to see, but
what God has originally breathed.
What I was designed to be.
With words embedded into my being,
I become transparent in black and white.
Unintentionally naked when I write.
Secrets hidden within my thighs, whisper in
between the pages.
Words escaping to leave my lips,
run to my hand and grip the pen,
until my quintessence transcends beyond the
paper and flows into hearts.
I have layers, Lovely.
Every smile has a message.
Every verbal sparse response
is filled with caged authenticity.
I was taught, unintentionally, how to
to live over cautiously and cater to my irrational fears.
To hold in my tears, because my sensitivity
was too heavy for the world to look at.
I used to sit on my own potential
faithfully.
Hiding my glow.
I woke up one morning,
not giving a rat's behind.

With fortitude in my eyes,
I busted out of my shell
and reunited with myself.
No longer afraid of my fragile essence
or my stern stances.
Not bothered by the perceptions of my fierce glances
and soft smiles.
Lovely, I want to introduce you to me.

Jazzy

My voice and its chill tone
is my silhouette.
You can't forget
me once I speak; you can't help but
become intrigued
by the lil lady
in Chuck Taylors
who named the pair Marie.
My lil switch doesn't declare
I'm in the room.
You're too swooned
by my smile.
Sucked in by my big heart
and kind words.
My genuine intentions
speak before I even part my lips.
No need to be tipped off
about what I stand for.
My motives are more transparent
than the core of a wine glass.
I just want to encourage, enlighten, and challenge the
malevolent to seek a safe resolve...
Intently involved with my own convictions
in addition, to seeking what breaks God's heart.
I'm a part of a clique that holds no
qualifications.
Just warriors who fought
diverse situations that should have executed

the sparkle in their eyes.
I don't demand the spotlight.
The world assumes I want it.
I'm just confident even in my flaws.
Why not flaunt them?
Why not let them know I hurt like *she* does
and get angry like *he* does?
Why not let them know that I believe in God for what He is now and
was?
   Sovereign.
Why not proclaim that we should all be in this together,
using my lil' ol' poems?
Why not show them there is no need to belittle another being
who bleeds the same deep blood red?
I just want to encourage, uplift and find beauty in
the cracks that were once closed.
I suppose heads held high are intimidating to heads hung low.
Nobody ever likes anyone so free and open with themselves. That's
why I'm so compelled to go against the grain
while, learning to love the fibers that are pulling on
the masterpiece I'm trying to create.
I'm aspiring to just be…

She

Soft smiles.
Penetrating eyes.
Fierce lips.
Gracious heart, yet defensive fingertips.
Hidden secrets and lost chances, give her more
reasons to dance with risk.
She kissed pessimism and got bit.
So now, she'll romance optimism until her dreams come into fruition.

A Somebody

I've always wanted to be a *somebody*.
Not a *anybody*.
Not a *everybody*.
A somebody.
See, the *everybodys* can't stand on their own.
Their prone to look like the masses.
They're drones.
They're clones.
Aiming to appear *normal and couth*.
Never standing out for their own good or for
the sake of humanity.
They ain't selfish-
       just scared.
Scared to live and scared to die.
Scared to chase their dreams
and afraid to openly cry.
"It's a sign of weakness", they say
as they hide in their comfort bubbles,
mumble over the stubble scraps of life
they have while, calling the *somebodys*
trouble.
Now the *anybodys* would do anything
for the limelight to sing down on their presence.
It's evident they always want to be seen.
Demean others with unique dreams while
tearing their loved ones at the seams.
Their agenda isn't to be vicious.
It's for attention.

There are dimensions to that thing.
Envying, coveting, stealing, and devouring
are just rain drops compared to the river
of conniving ideas to get everybody's eyes and ears.
Too bad the *anybodys* are too blind to see
that their attention hogging schemes,
will only abandon them to feel more
hallow then before.
But, the *somebodys*
just want to embrace themselves.
They're compelled to find where their heart abides.
Never hide or live in shame when change knocks on their door.
They're confident in their funkiness.
Bold enough to stand alone.
Always, they stand tall.
Quick to get low
and eternally receptive to growth.
They're not cocky.
Their uniqueness has no room to boast.
No need to gloat over what God gave them.
No need to bring down another being
who bleeds the same as them.
No need for a spotlight,
they already shine like neon lights,
even in the daylight.
Often misunderstood
and they consistently go against the grain.
Some *somebodys* are even labeled insane
by attempting to reform torn apart
practices.
But they keep strutting.

Keep striving.
Keep going.
They continue to show the world what
different looks like, without even trying.
Without even the desire to be seen.
They can't help but be seen.
I wanna be a *somebody*.

Sandra

Sandra got
big beautiful brown eyes
that can smile, laugh
cry and endure through anything.
Her eyes speak words
of hope to cope through
life's storms.

Sandra got a laugh
that goes beyond the artificial joys of this world.
She got that
"The joy of the Lord is my strength"
kinda laugh,
the
"I'm happy, happy in Jesus"
kinda laugh.

Sandra got
Xena The Warrior Princess strength.
Nah,
she got that Foxy Brown- Pam Grier
strength.
Nah,
she on some Joan of Arc status.

Sandra is a queen
like Nefertiti
Nah,

she is Cleopatra.
She is Esther.
Sandra is,
Queen Ma of all mommies;
she is amazingly humble and strong enough
to hold down a city.
She can conquer hearts with her order
and blue-jay persona.
Sandra is strict.
A gnat can't pass her by sly
without her telling it
to fly straight.
Sandra can debate.
She'll wait for your perspective but
then she'll override it and cunningly
place you on a better direction.
(Really her direction)

Sandra got hands
that have been seasoned with divine
spices and herbs.
That have carried life's joys and pains.
Hands that have
taught, preached, fed, bathed, loved
nurtured, held, worked, fought, prayed and
so much more.
Hold her hand.
Take a tour and glide through her experiences.

Sandra is so silly.
She ain't no boring square.
      Sandra is a star shaped

personality that loves an invisible being and is a witness to His grace.
Her place on this earth is identified
as:
daughter, sister, friend, preacher and mother.
Sandra is a mother.
      The kind of mother
that their only child would write poems about.
      Kind of like this one.

He Still Remains

He still calls me Princess
and reminds me of my worth.
He's always changing internally.
Transforming to who he's supposed to be,
while extracting the lessons of who he
once was.
He's got enough wisdom to beat
the monks to their "core".
Endurance is his preservation.
Giving up is never a temptation;
faith is a must.
He's got substance.
Accepts all and tolerates nothing under respect.
Doesn't neglect my ache but soothes
my post adolescent with encouragement.
He's my Daddy.
He looks like an older brother
and
still looks out for my mother.
Although they never married,
there were times he carried her through storms.
He was never the thorn or a statistic to leave.
He came in my life and remains.
As life has changed and we both caused each other aches,
he still remains.
Some things still cause me pain and I have to accept
parts of him that'll never change.
I still remain.
As the years have passed and secrets have been

revealed,
I feel some ugliness could have been concealed.
We still remain.
When all the pain ceases and all the dust settles, his love continues.
It's untainted.
Unshaken.
He's confident in my growth.
He's more understanding than most.
Never startled by my mistakes, but smiles
at my ability to move forward.
Wisdom and all.
Love and acceptance.
Open minded with contentment,
he remains.

Letter to My Confidant

Dedicated to Rebecca Preval

Dear Confidant,

Don't hide your innocence when the wicked perceive
your integrity as obsolete.
The ashes of your past tears will rise up
like a phoenix and soar passed
their petty expectations of you.
Your naivety is see through like
vintage glass vases pierced by the sunlight.
The world can't handle your beauty.
The world isn't ready for your beauty.
But, your loved ones are receptive
to your smile, your caring agenda and
bashful utterances.
You speak softly when unsure and bodacious
when your confidence is pure.
I'll concur with the outsiders that your
physical appearance is favorable.
In my terms, *My bestie is dope and fantastic.*
Your style is a splash of funk with a shoe box
full of bombastic confidence.
There's little
care for naysayers whispering to itchy ears.
You're too busy transforming into the
colorful butterfly Queen you're meant to be.

Please,
remember to wear your crown properly
as the insecure attempt
to belittle your royalty.
Don't be afraid to release your
identity from your lips to the serpents
that arrogantly place their hands
on their hips, with dignity the
size of Doritos chips.
Intimidation comes in many ways.
Sometimes as hate.
Sometimes as envy.
Learn to grow tough wings before it's
too late and you're set in your ways.
Flutter through the painful moments
and when you make a mistake, own it.

Dear Confidant,

I appreciate your constant reminders that I need to slow down.
That it's imperative to cease frowning at my traits that
cause others to be encouraged.
I admire our awkwardness that fits well into our
triangle that's shaped into an octagon.
You weren't called to be a slight breeze roaming
through this earth, Confidant.
I treasure the days you realize that.
I will continue to remind you on the days
you forget.

I Love You, Friend

Dedicated to Keneil Buchanan

We.
We walk the same direction, but different sidewalks.
We're always in the same season,
just different reasons as to how we saw the first snowflake,
or the first flower bloom or why I'm being pushed by this
bully-feeling wind.
We're outcasts that found each other in the middle
of our, *unicorn-dragon mission.*
We're positioned to hold each other's worlds like the Atlas god.
I know that now.

My irrational fears kiss my
dreams like lovers on *"Honey Moon Night."*
But you're never frightened by my
dangerous hesitations to chase what my heart
is meant for.
I know that now.
I know that you're a confidant that
royalty such as King David had.
The kind that will grab my hand right before I jump
into my own chaos and remind me
that we are made to burn and revive like phoenixes.
I'm blessed.

Your smile…
Rough cheekbones and dense facial features,

even the grim reaper pauses at your mean mug.
But, your smile,
is wealthier than billionaires residing
within the fresh breezes of their own islands.
Even in the silence of our conversations I can
hear your grin.
Hear it hum consistency, awkwardness
with a short melody of awesomeness.
I love you, friend.
Samson ain't go nothin' on your resilience you've obtained overnight.
Empathy heaves in the crevices of your embrace,
as I preach to you my pessimism like biblical scriptures.
You are an elixir of patience and understanding
leaking, overflowing from the table onto my lap.
No need to clean this up.
Let it stain.
Please, stain.
Soak in.

With your silent declarations of love,
I still wonder how you preside amongst my core with confidence.
Accepting all my flaws like gold and killing my doubts with truth.
With truth that I am still scared to let soak in.
You're far from simple, nothing is under-perplexed and not to be labeled.
I hope fables are birthed about us.
Friend, united, we are unicorn riders and
dragons that can disintegrate galaxies if they come

between us.
We taste like victory before the sunrises.
We are blatant weirdos that chastise insensitivity
and grieve when our favorite characters, in books, die.
We are the heroes of our imagination.
We're the story behind exhortation.

I love you, friend.

Andrea

Hey lil mama,
Your awesomeness is leaking at the seams
and it seems you're too blind to notice the
shine glistening from your sides.
Can't see your potential 'cause the
night sky is covering your eyes.
The stars are trying to remind you
that you're just like them:
brightening the beautiful darkness
for those who want to see its mystery.
Please receive this poem as a message saying:
I'm praying that you boldly step
on the pressures of this world and coil
them around your fingers like
tight Shirley Temple curls.
I think I'll always identify you
as, the friend with the most moxy and
care.
As the woman who prides in
her sensitivity and outlasts
the storms with grace and longevity.
The struggle has not grasped you.
You've snatched it by its collar.
You didn't even bother to wipe its nose,
as it whimpers with regret from ever
trying to cross your path.
You'll triumph, lil mama, like you always do.
Like foxy 1930's ladies who sass their
way into the speak easies and

bare the heaviest burden with class.
It will all pass...
I promise it will all pass.
Don't let the world dim out your sparkle that
lights up the dead eyes and your laugh
that hypes up the hesitant.
Don't discipline your platinum presence,
or trade in your voice for surrendered defeat.
Yes, your awesomeness is leaking from the seams
but I think it's evidence of what is to come...
It's your story beating out the cold from hearts like
a lambeg drum.

Poetry Is…

Poetry is a natural high.
Better than old men peace-piping on a hot summer day
while watching the kids play on the wet concrete
as the fire hydrant sprays.
Better than an ocean breeze breathing past your face
as neo-soul is clogged in your ears.
You see, poetry is music
internal rhymes, rhythm and blues
from the abyss of our beings.
Poetry is like a willow tree.
Weeping many styles and voices.
Its limbs urge to speak words you ain't ever heard jumbled up before.
Go on-
chop it down.
You'll see the voices come together and start
growing at the roots, branching out stanzas from different lives and
every leaf will scream out imagery.
They will influence your heart to feel feelings you ain't ever felt
before.
Poetry drowns the soul
with acoustic vibes from someone's footsteps.
They breathe them into your emotions, have you boasting
because you got a piece of that passion
that no one can steal.
But, you can listen.
You can watch.

You can watch the words conquer the blank paper,
allow it to touch your spirit.
Dare to understand
and relate to the writer's pain
 joy, peace and transformation.
            Poetry is temptation.
Enticing you to open up your mind.
Tempting you to be vulnerable
enough to be heartbroken, because she is
and
to be angry, because he is.
Tempting you to go past reality.
An escape that chases away your own personal chaos.
            Poetry is a natural high.
Better than old men peace piping on a hot summer day
while watching kids play on the wet concrete,
as the fire hydrant sprays to cool everybody down.

Determined

Addicted to my thoughts,
my high is my imagination.
Slick talk isn't temptation
unless you're saying something.
Haughty lines won't seduce
me to define what you see in me.
My demeaning reality won't
deject my goals.
My flight of fancy will soon unfold.
Tell me some absolute truth untold
and maybe my defiant aggression
wouldn't be so bold.
Addicted to my thoughts,
my high is my imagination.
Slick talk isn't temptation
unless you're saying something.
Not moved by your foxy talk
or pessimistic hogwash.
I'm enticed by these dragons in my head
dreading for me to quit.
Interested in the humble pie with its pie crust lips telling me to,
"never forget this!"
Addicted to my thoughts,
my high is my imagination.
Drugs, alcohol and sex ain't close to my thought's sedation.

Dead Thoughts

Dead thoughts reveal themselves
right before I go to sleep
like a forgotten task.
An overcast of skeletal images and banged up
mistakes will awake from their slumber.
They creep in my mind, find ways
to rehash the days, I swore I forgot
and I know I've forgiven.
I surrender to my ancient corpses, filled with anger.
Those dead thoughts whisper, "How you livin'?"
I shake my head and remember
those dead thoughts are deceased for a reason.
And, I won't miss them.

I Apologize

I'm sorry
if my smile deceived you to believe that I am adjacent to tissue paper.
Use me then, flush me away.
You'd say the sweetest things
filled with candy lies dressed in faux mink jackets.
Keep your plastic friendship-
I'm better off minus one.
Better off without pretty smiles and false care.
Go on, wear your faux mink jacket with its lying lining inside.
Hopefully, your manipulation will keep you warm when the world
grows cold toward you.

Strutting Freedom

I will nevermore be afraid
of the dark.
I won't fear his venomous silence
that whispered violation
into the crevasses of my being.
        I will no longer hate him.
I won't fear his hands, running through
a bed of roses that keel over, way after
his shadow has left its presence.
Nevermore, will I shiver at his petty retaliations
and rot a little at the core.
        I have been reborn.
I snatched away the vicious storms
that blew hail
and immensely pricked my confidence like thorns.
        I am healing now.
No matter how hard he threatens to keel over
my bed of roses,
God will ascend His strength
like rain upon my being.
I will never more be afraid
of walking alone, with black corpses
laying in my mind.
He probably thought he held me down for good.
Maybe he should look back
at the ashes.
I am a phoenix.

Ms. King David

Burning within and bleeding even deeper.
Keeper of my soul,
please fold all of this misery.
Annihilate its being.
I am screaming.
So loud in my mind, the kind words of my lover sound barren and
cold.
His words drop in mid-air and I'm left alone.
Stranded in my own world of madness.
I am **not** okay.
Screaming so loud, but only my veins can hear it.
Holy spirit, please rain down your peace, your comfort and joy.
My ending wants to come too soon and I think I am about to blow
up,
erupt, leave no remains.
I need a change.
Maybe tangible happiness or peaceful solitude.
Through with these deafening whispers
of glumness.
I am done with this.
Lord, relentlessly chase me out
of this wilderness.

Raw

Don't talk to me about my *destiny*
when the recipe of my eviction notice is cookin' in the oven.
I'm fixin' to be served hot while you still fussin' about the clothes I got.
Jobs don't drop from trees.
If they did, I wouldn't be in this wilderness being
stung by the bees and choked by negativity.
Excuse the ripeness of the fruit
I'm bearing.
I guess my heart's not a fan of
dodging the truth.
I'm not amused neither do I find it cute to snatch struggle from my
lips due to my youth.
"YOUR SEASON IS NOW!"
what?
Sit down.
Right now, I'm Ms. King David
before the crown.
Daniel when he was down
in the lion's den
and Joseph when he was sent to prison.
Listen, I'm in a dark place and I won't trace around my reality-
but, I'll keep walking and following
that little glow in the distance.
Become the unique me despite the churchy resistance.
Become relentless in gratitude; meditate the beatitudes,
while feeling for my dreams in the darkness.

I won't deny my pain with scriptures out of place-
but have faith that everything will fall into place,
while chasing who God called me to be.
I won't receive what you speak into existence.
        You are not the creator.
I will not cater to denial nor ignore the thunder outside
of my house.
The .45 caliber never sounded so eerie when its
bullet's pierce a child.
I won't go wild about a conference about finding
my destiny when I think my own persona is my enemy.
When a girl named Stefani doesn't see how
beautiful she is naturally.
Excuse my transparency.
I guess I'm not a fan of placing stones
on those who are casualties of this cold world.
I actually believe my Savior thinks outside
of your boxes and my own.
My behavior isn't uncouth.
It is my human illuminating.
I will not ignore the truth that life has
its ups and downs.
No matter how charismatically profound
your words may seem.
I won't demean this pit I'm in-
I've been weaned off of storm-denial
for a while now.
I'll trust God during these dark hours
and embrace my tears.
Embrace my frustrations with power
saying,

"Weeping may endure for a night
but joy cometh in the morning."
I will stare my woeful heart in the face
and chase away defeat from my
heart's beat.
Don't attempt to remedy my native emotions
just because they aren't
sunbathing in bliss.
I've chosen to kiss every season softly
knowing all the rain and sunshine is needed
for the beautiful rose that I am to become.

This Feeling

A vintage feeling discreetly creeps beneath
my sheets and into my veins.
A change in the air stares me in the face, knowing
I can't chase it away.
I'm awakened.
I blink once and cry twice as hard as I did
when this feeling was fresh and bright.
I thought I was blessed.
I am stressed now that my heart screams anguish.
My eyes are being attacked intentionally during my time-
my moment of weakness.
How do I face this despairing spirit?
I hear it in my mind, searching for my thoughts that insinuate
optimism
and destroy it.
I hate this.
This feels like a storm with thorns pricking at my emotions and
killing
me within.
Have I greatly sinned?
What have I done to be burdened with
a feeling so dark, so morose?
I thought I chose bliss.

Tides

Something inside me told me to scream.
      It was too late.
The tides were already rushing in, engulfing me with corpses
that died at age sixteen.
      Something told me to scream.
When I saw those snowflakes…
Felt them numb my eyelids and purify my lashes.
      Suddenly, flashes of the past conquered me,
blinding me from the scriptures and sermons.
Surpassed the sunny days and cherished moments.
      Something in the abyss of my soul told me to scream-
      as I never have screamed before.
I prayed for solace way before the beginning of the waves.
How am I supposed to behave
when my mind is unwillingly a slave
to these corpses?
I prayed for freedom since the flashbacks and overflowing fears.
Way before the tears were more frequent than breathing.
      Something immersed into my being urged me to cry out.
To bring about a plan to withstand the rushing waters
and drenched agony.
These skeletons pierce my thoughts like
victorious arrows from the Pequot.
Something embedded in my spirit begged me to scream-
      scream until the on-lookers would
reach out a hand or dive in to save me.
I've been humming "I Need Thee" way before
the waves came crashing in.
Before the red smears appeared.
Before the fear of drowning became a fear.
      Am I humming in vain?
Will this stain of shame ever be removed?
I have no choice but to soothe my pain with

disdained happiness and schizophrenic logic.
     Something behooved me to clamor
until I retrieved my voice again.
I have been screaming before the tides…
When will it all end?

Relapses

Relapses.
Rehashing old habits
to cope with new cold chills
that eradicate future promises with one blow to the gut.
Excuse me if my season of, *being in a rut* causes you to flinch.
The dangerous stench that's in the air whispers soft lines written
on places no one is allowed to see.
In the dark, is where I used to shine brightly
so, I'll return to what I know.
Relapses.
Shame igniters that kiss me after the *aftermath regrets*
so softly, I forget the violent addiction.
But my actions gave me the predictions I'd be
meeting the darkness again.
As I continue to pretend to the masses that I'm not in demise,
my soul whimpers old pains and fresh ones that can't
leave my lips.
The tip of my caste iron heart is bending.
Relapses.
Making gold smiles melt into
puddles of defeat as discreet
habits cause guilt to run deep.
Nothing is more humiliating than facing
old corpses.

Relapses.
Snatching away hope
and reminding me of the vintage ways to cope.
But it's too old-
I've already scoped through
fresh ways to kill this painful vibe.
Already been good for so long.
So then, why am I still humming an old song?
Why I am wondering if I belong?
Relapses.

2am Prayer

Lord,
open my mouth to reveal my testimonies.
But, first remove shame from the depths of me.
Bring out the shattered parts of my voice
and mold it for your glory.
Allow my stories to break yokes
and transform my trauma to hope.
Help the broken hearted to become receptive,
so they can gain wisdom without thinking I have wicked incentives.
I just don't want my pain to be in vain.
Just don't want the broken chains to be forgotten,
or the one who unlocked it.
Jesus, set the captives free and place their
pain in your pocket and your peace in their hearts.
Allow my flow to glow brightly because of your presence.
Allow it to draw people to true benevolence.
Help me to stand out like you called me to be.
Help me make amends with my pain, so you can bring about its
beauty.
Chase after the deeply hurting, relentlessly, until they surrender whole
heartedly.
Whisper in their ears; you were yearning for them constantly.
Always remind them that you died to be their remedy
and rose to walk in deliverance with them.
Allow my struggles to relatively pierce their minds to find
you before they're out of time.
Amen.

Hope

Seeping through the cracks,
      barely pushing through the concrete.
Discreet fears hide beneath my eyes,
      so I lie and say I'm okay as my roots shrivel up,
sinking back into the concrete.
    My integrity is long gone,
      lost within the grave next to peace and serenity.
        I have become my own enemy.
Where is the remedy?
…Quietly,
a breeze
passes through my chest and
beneath my heart-
and hushes my core.
Roots begin to grow fat.
Spontaneous waters flow through
as I begin to ponder future victories.

Talking Shells

My heart was boldly illuminating under the sun
and bathing in its beauty.
Captivated by the world, and its
delight in what I thought was
reality.
My heart was naively transparent
to the devious shells that rested next
to my emotions.
Verbally potent, those shells reminded me
that life without risks is no life at all.
So, I must allow my heart to feel and embrace
the chance of getting hurt.
I received the pain and still remain
on this shore.
However, my heart isn't facing the sun anymore.

Fear

Holding on to what looks to be good,
knowing I should
 let it go,
let it flow to the river of sin.
I begin to realize the wrongs
that feel so sweet aren't so sweet.
I greet it at the door saying:
"Once more shall we bond again?"
I know this will lead to regret
and painful daydreams.
But, it seems I'm addicted.
I can't leave it alone,
I'm prone to it.
Am I a slave to it?
As blessed as I am,
I stand by the pit of temptation
 and without hesitation I whisper,
"Once more shall we bond again?"
I pretend to be naive and receive it, breathing in its venom.
Then, a sour taste like lemons fills my heart's mouth.
Suddenly, reality annihilates the false sugars of it.
I'm hit hard by the truth.
It is evil in disguise,
screaming out lovely lies,
looking so sweet to the eye.
Look deeper.
It's the shadow of the reaper.

I greet it at the door crying out,
"Never more shall your venom
spill in my mind;
nevermore will we intertwine
becoming one."
It slowly fades away,
but still seeps around the mind of those willing to accept it.
I'm set free from its captivity.
But, for how long?
'til my heart's willing to see it as a remedy?
Never again.

Courage

I wanna kiss the stars during the daytime
and tell 'em I could still see 'em.
Whisper to 'em my dreams
and my regrets.
I don't have any yet.
But, as time projects from my
dark circles and responsibilities,
I think I'll have a list.
I want them stars to answer me back
and tell me that life is bigger than my mistakes.
It's bigger than my hesitations.
It's about reaching all my destinations
with crazy stories about the voyage there.

If You Let Me

If you let me,
I'd kiss your scars
with lips that drip
of a remedy close to perfection.
I want those wounds.
I don't want to swoon you with sweet nothings.
I'd rather you depart from me with more
clarity in your eyes.
I want the sides of you that your heart won't
allow you to reveal.
I'd peel away the regrets that force
your eyes to blink twice as hard
and feel just as low…
If you let me.
Blow serenity over the inner parts
that nobody has seen.
I want your safe routines.
I'd caress your fears of the unknown
and tickle your goals with curiosity's opioid
so potently, you won't comprehend
what a comfort zone is.
I want your hesitations of pursing the night sky.
I want your vulnerability on its knees,
so I can retrieve the keys to your
core and
snatch the ache from your heart.

Impart joy to your soul, unfold your
happiness and pour it down your spine.
Cut off the toxic vines that latched to your
dreams, with an axe made by
the sun's essence.
Tease your intellect to leave its
hiding place and let the world
ameliorate from its
intricate ideas.
I want your everything.
If you let me...
I'd rub tranquility into your
hands and demand
anxiety to flee from your
existence.
I'd roll with you through life
with resilience.
If you let me...

Mr. Long Lashes

Mr. Long Lashes,
you've got eyes that reveal stories from your past.
So, intrigued by what they say, I ain't shocked
I fell so fast.
I easily looked past the obvious and ventured
into what was hidden.
Thought thoughts that were forbidden.
Gazed deeply into the stories those pupils told
and made sure my heart took notes.
I'm in this deep and boastfully losing sleep.
Late night thoughts of you and "what if" scenarios.
Voice stays playing in my head like Marten Coltrane stereos.
Ain't scared of this anymore, you give me no reason to be.
You bit down into my naive glances and timid embraces.
You treat me like I'm imperative; I sometimes wonder how that
could be.
A perfect ten like you, seeing all my flaws, I was sure you'd withdraw.
Yet, you gaze at me in awe, think I'm gorgeous even with a head scarf
on.
Not a fan of boxes.
I'm an octagon
that encourages the sheepish to shine through.
One who will be openly honest with you.
Dust off some of those burdens and
and heal a few wounds too.
Honored you're interested in lil' ol' me, I just hope you don't get tired
of me.

My Quintessence

You got long lashes with eyes that tattle tell
on the stories you'd never tell.
I'm in this deep and I'm boastfully losing sleep.
late night thoughts of you, and "what if" scenarios.
Voice stay playing in my head like Marten Coltrane stereos.

Trademarked Butterflies

I want to be the one
who trademarks those butterflies in your stomach.
The reason behind those long winded
gazes out the train window, the long pauses you make when you
realize someone looks past your outward
"swag" and observes your warm persona.
I want to go back in time to the moment
I snatched a hug before I darted into that cab.
I'd break the hour glass and
make that moment timeless.
Hold that moment.
Own it like self-made millionaires
and their assets.
If only…
I'd be lying if I told you
I forget to mention you in prayer and care not for
your wellbeing.
I'd be deceiving myself if I told you
I don't ponder the "what ifs".
Did anyone ever tell you that your eyes are innocently inviting,
slightly luring everyone into its tales?
Your grin gives no mercy as I
unwillingly curtsy at your charm.
I'm never alarmed by your embraces or
shudder at your outbursts…
My thoughts seem to linger back to the
last time I saw you enter the room.
Hands jammed in your pockets,

like you had nothing to prove.
Not guarded-
just separated from distraction.
Purposely I ceased my reflection and embraced
my sickness of jittery hands and warm cheek bones;
Kool-aid smiles and the moment of being accident prone.
I intercede for you, with passion aside and love as my guide.
I intercede for you.
Passion aside, but 1Corinthians 13:4 as my guide.
I want to be the one who trademarks those butterflies in
your stomach.
But I'll be at peace if I'm not, because you being an inspiration
for me is more than enough.

My Favorite Broken Heart

I don't care where we're going,
even if it's crashing and burning.
I'm only yearning to live in this moment.
I appreciate the gift of our leveled communication, shy hesitations,
soft glances and passionate intentions.
Our cores meet eye to eye and
I'd be lying if I didn't tell the world this truth:
You'll be my favorite broken heart.
No, I don't fall apart from the aching fact.
I'm too blinded by your transparency and soft holds.
Our interaction unfolds to the world like gold leaves falling during a
summer blackout.
         I don't care about the green monsters witnessing something
they've never felt.
 I don't mind our different perspectives that should inevitably clash.
         Yet, somehow when we get together, we always seem to
mesh.
 I don't care about your imperfections.
I've embraced them all without hesitation.
However, I'm aware of our destination and I knew from the start,
that you'll be my by favorite broken heart.
I'm not being pessimistic, just embracing the truth
that you're
feelings are not as deep as mine are for you.
No remedy to this.
Except to ride out our moment together until the

wheels fall off.
I know it will cost my heart and a bit of my emotions,
but I'm already coasting on how you make me feel.
I don't care about what the naysayers reveal.
I refuse to deal with the truth that the concept of us is only
temporary.
     - 'Cause, this moment feels legendary.

Abrupt

I fell hard.
Hit my face on the pavement
after kissing reason and gravity goodbye.
The "what ifs" and memories still linger in hidden cries.
I laid there-
looking for your hand to clutch mine.
I cried when you didn't grasp for my grip.
I couldn't comprehend how you didn't land right beside me.
Until I saw you standing in the distance,
with your ego firmly planted around
your feet.
I understand.
Your hands were full.
They were carrying wounds and over crowed thoughts that you
entertained,
until you were deranged with pain and heart ache.
That's why you couldn't help but
let my heart break.

Façade

You were poetry in motion.
A wicked potion I toasted to the violent tides
before sipping you down.
You made me the clown that everyone shined they're pity   towards.
I'm trying to move forward, but you keep
leaving little pastries on my kitchen table.
Just give me the truth so I can be stable.
Originally, you were painted bright red
and everything you said
sounded stern-
crystal clear like Grandma's good chandelier,
that hung in the living room.
Oh, how it shined.
Such intricate details and the memories it entailed underneath its
charm.
Oh, how I fell for your charm.
That bashful charm.
But, one can only fabricate goodness but for so long.
You scammed me well.
Rolled the dice on my heart like low lives playing craps.
Just don't leave me trapped.

Hidden Agendas

You had the balls to show me your wounds,
but no audacity to tell me the truth.
Maybe this is karma in a lover's suit.
I salute your rendition of a gentleman,
your kind words smothered with venom
and
your agenda that was so greatly hidden,
I'm sure you couldn't even find back then.
I was a *challenge*.
You couldn't manage to understand
that these sexy long legs weren't
quick to spread like shoppers on Black Friday.
They say good things come to those who wait.
But you came in someone else and
cursed patience in the face.
You had the guts to reveal the dark corners of your heart,
yet skimped on the spunkiness to keep it real.
I should have concealed my own wounds.
I revealed nothing less of my quintessence,
shared precious secrets without question.
But it seems sexy post-adolescence was the only
thing that could get your attention.
You couldn't comprehend that my standards
were not for pretend.
Baby, I'm not some cheap buffet.
I'm a dope bombastic ruby, an unconventional beauty,
and a lovely lady just trying to walk in integrity.
You claimed I was what you wanted but really,

you desired ejaculations that left you breathlessly anticipating
another round.
So glad I'm over you now.
My Grandpa would have been proud.

Brick Hearted Fellow

Your sexual consumption and empty emotions,
have resulted in your presumptuous idea that your wound healed
long ago.
Dear brick hearted fellow,
your rationality is now your foe.
You've repetitively chased down your inference and kissed it with
plastic.
With your hands shaking and your heart breaking, you kissed it with
plastic.
I guess facing the truth would've been too drastic.
I just wanted to be there for you.
I challenged you to reason with the idea that maybe-
just maybe,
your heart is still dancing with corpses that deceived you.
Now, in return, you reject anyone who receives you.
I just wanted to be there for you.
You seek after authentic souls, yet give into sham hearts
that surrender nothing substantial, but they visually feel whole.
Dear brick hearted fellow,
why fear what you wanted and hate what you submitted to?
Why run when you are challenged, but fight for idleness?
Why hand me thorns after I introduced kindness?
I just wanted to be there for you.
The bitter taste in your mouth will remain a trademark for your
stagnant strides and lost choices.

I just wanted to be one of the voices you listened to when the world
entices you to drink its poison.
But,
you're too busy dancing with deceit while discreetly disgracing other
hearts that only see their value as a single digit.
I'll cease to fidget at your responses or wave red flags in your
direction.
I'll watch you sink sadly with your
unsatisfied erection, empty affection, resentful dancing and
stamped bitterness.
I just wanted you to be happy.
I just wanted to be there.
Nonetheless, my simple request was too heavy
for such a wounded soul.
Oh, you brick hearted fellow.
So, blinded by what once was,
you can't see what should be.

Dead Butterflies

I got these dead butterflies in the pit of my stomach.
But I swear they're still alive
        they're just too scared to fly.
Hesitant to flutter naively past your plastic words coated with honey.
Honey, I really thought we were gonna be
bodacious lovers living on soft glances and tough back bones.
But,
you're prone to turn to your past like she'll be your last
and your heart holds her hand.
I do understand.
But,
you can't sail towards the new land if you're still leeching on the old
land's sand.
Listen, I got these dead butterflies in the abyss of my tummy.
But,
I swear they're still fluttering at your deceitful promises and lost time.
Time, something that you initially had for me.
But,
as time made you face your fear, you steered that ship left when I was
still focused on going right.
Right towards something bigger than what your doubts could
comprehend.
But,

I won't pretend like I didn't see the hints.
Despite your "No, I'm still interested"
Your actions whispered to me
"He's no longer in this, Kid."
I really thought we could be bodacious lovers living on soft glances
and old school romance.
But,
you're so bound up in the corpses, you can't take the chance.
No need for a last dance-
I'm gone.

Those Darn Butterflies

I don't regret a thing.
It's just, sometimes I wish I would've
torn those butterflies wing by wing,
once I felt the fluttering,
once I started stuttering after hearing
you release sweet nothings to me.

Better Without You

You made it crystal clear.
Nevertheless,
my eyes simulated your *authenticity*,
even though
your heart revealed atrocities
more wicked than Pol Pot's philosophies.
I was blinded.
Intentionally threw my heart in a blood red sea, hoping
it was sweet tropic blue.
I front like I didn't give you vulnerable parts of my mind.
Like I'm not scared that letting you go would put me in a bind.
Like I wasn't inclined to receive your
rapacious ways.
Like I wasn't receptive to the new you, despite its poisonous
attributes.
I would love to say that I am not in love with you.
I want to declare that I'm better without you.
But I can't seem to believe such a veracious utterance.
There's so much substance in, "I'm better without you."
So much love for myself in, "I'm better without you."
I don't need your help in, "I'm better without you."
I will no longer be put on your shelf in, "I'm better without you."
At least I found my worth yet again.

Following the hard to gulp down truth of your shady,
180° degree
transitions.
At least I walked away with tears flowing, dignity still whole
and empty hands.
I still don't understand what happened.
Occasionally haunted with *what if* thoughts and silent replies.
I want to declare that I'm better without you.
I **need** to declare that I'm better without you.
But I can't seem to believe such a veracious utterance.
There's so much substance in, "I'm better without you."
So much love for my own self in, "I'm better without you."
I don't need your help in, "I'm better without you."
I will no longer be put on your shelf in, "I'm better without you."
Oh, I will someday.
With my hands on my hips and my heart guarded on a
steel pedestal
Once the fool, I'll wisely declare that I'm better without you.
For now, I'll drape my emotions with strength and
heal with the support of loved ones.
Funny, I thought you would be one of them.

Neon Hints and Bold Signs

I embodied our yesterdays like
vintage prose in anthologies.
Probably since apologies are never
in order for our skeletons.
I stood between your wounds
and
the softest part of your essence.
      I understand…
You couldn't see the authenticity
in my switch,
couldn't catch the hints in my quintessence.
It was evident to the world
I just wanted your core.
But you craved more hints
to hush your irrational fears.
I embodied every part of you
like cocoons to caterpillars.
Did you at least consider the motions
my heart was making?
I watched your walls slowly disintegrate
and rebuild once I saw
the raw parts of your presence.
      I get it…
You couldn't discern my yearning
to embrace the dark corners of you
too.
You couldn't see my neon actions,
tattooed on my forearms that read,
"I love you."

Unnecessary Lines and Abrupt Conclusions

Captured the "what ifs" following the
twinkling of the last page in our book.
Fell in love with your character
after the first chapter,
without a morning after.
I was hooked after reading our
preface.
I premised our book would end at the crevice
of infinity.
Or, maybe in the middle of your last
breath or mine.
Your eyes still run in my mind like
time-
never ceasing or slowing down.
I'm drowned within our book.
Re-reading passages until I get to the end.
After, I'll pretend as though
I'm not anticipating a sequel.
Smirk with the people as though
I'm over our memoir.
When really, I'm dying to be a part of
your repertoire and last song.
Nonetheless, I won't interrupt the morning glory
you're voyaging to be written in your
masterpiece.
You've been deprived of it since the beginning of
your own story.
I'm at peace with knowing
there is something about us on your bookshelf.

Clear

I meant every word I said.
Every naked affection.
No regrets disclosing my
fearful directions, stupid choices
and hidden imperfections.
I gave my heart to you-
in total perfection.
Blindly felt for the cookie crumbs to your heart.
Took heed to the seeds that were
once held by past
lovers and friends that made
no amends for their intentions,
no shame to their wicked agendas.
I desired-
I still desire to reach your core,
adore each crack, each flaw
and passion.
Drown compassion on the cold parts.
Decline to depart from your heart,
until divine skies over cast your eyelids
and winter settles into your flesh.
My intentions were naïve and authentic,
without any hesitation to wander.
I didn't ponder the actual conclusion
that your lips revealed nothing but allusions.
But, I did consider the dangers.
Aware that I could endanger my heart in return for nothing more
than cherished memories

and bittersweet endings.
I was still nothing more than genuine
and I don't regret a thing
I'm glad for the fling.
Just hurt at your latter actions and interactions.
I was nothing more than genuine.
I still desire to reach your core
and adore each crack, each flaw, each glow and passion.
Drown compassion on the cold parts and never depart
from your heart until divine skies overcast
your eyelids and winter settles
into your flesh.
I wish you all the best.

KeeKee

This is an ode to your authenticity
that I can still taste on my tongue.
Closure never tasted so bitter.
It slithered down my throat like
ice coffee to workaholic junkies.
         I still have the munchies
for your essence.
Still yearn for your presence no
matter how you're feeling.
I'd rather be in the kitchen peeling off
the irrational fears we both concluded
as *realistic.*
We're the same person ya know,
just different lives.
You were too blind to see that
I would've stood beside you, despite
the cloudy skies and smoldering kitchen.
I strived to make you aware of that.
That I'd slash through your defenses like
ancient samurais and ease your
heartaches with good salves church mothers
used to make.
That I'd take your tensions and stretch it out
to the heavens to remind God that
you're down here and need some guidance.
I would've have stayed even in the daunting silence.
I dedicate this poem to the confusion we now
share and the pride we hold to *protect* us from clarity.
And, to the hesitations we cling on to like
Viking shields to protect our hearts from something
as real as hope...

Mushy

When you were drenched with tension or pressure was tight
on you like the skin on a grape,
I wanted to be the source of your motivation to keep busting
through the odds.
I wanted to be that gold leaf that fell from the
shady trees in front of your feet
that you'd pick up and hold tightly until
the best outcomes came to your mind,
played on repeat.
When you felt stuck and surrendered to the lie
that you were a failure,
I wanted to be one of the voices in your heart that
always cheered you on.
I wanted to be that song that made you dance without
your mental consent.
I just wanted to protect your heart.
Not reject your everything like some cheap manufactured
goods we Americans faithfully overprice.
I wanted to cease your skepticism that nobody could really embrace
all the dark corners, as well as the brightly
lit places in your heart.
When the night sky felt like it was placed on your shoulders and
the moon light was nowhere to be found to
guide you,
I wanted to be the constellation

to assist your footsteps.
Just wanted to be
the rudder on your sailboat as you ride the treacherous waves,
the rainbow after your storms,
the reason why you wanted to pull out your hair,
the fire that ignited your desire to change for the better,
the hot feeling in your cheeks when you were bashful.
Darn, I even wanted to be the culprit as to why your nerves flew off
the walls.
We should return for the curtain call and possibly
perform another encore.
Too bad our cores are pushed with too much pride
to disclose our honesty.

I Miss That You

I gave you too much attention.
There were dimensions to that thing.
I'd wake up serenading your name to the constellations at 3am,
hoping my heart's desire of your presence would come to pass.
Your eyes used to gaze at me like I was the
Sirius Star and you were the telescope.
I don't want to cope with the idea that I'm no
longer a part of your night sky.
That you'll nevermore be the source of my random
smiles, when I'm alone.
Your eyes adored me
like I was the medley and you were the listening fan.
Your eyes adored me.
Nevertheless,
that was back when you and I were fresh lovers wanting,
to dig deeper in each other's souls
until we found our cores.
I miss *that* you.
Nevertheless, I'll honor the memories.
Hold tightly to the moments you gave me.
I'll hold them firm and cautiously.
I'll write words that dance on the pages of my mind
and
one day disclose those words to the masses.
I miss *that* you.

Illusions

This delicate face of mine.
You liked the idea of me.
Loved the Jasmine that
resided in your dreams.
Appreciated my high cheekbones that beamed
faithfulness and screamed peace.
Favored my soft eyes that whispered
countless stories about some glory days and
my silly ways.
You deceived me to receive your sham sincerity.
I believed the fairytales you released from your lips.
You soothed my wounds with
your candied words and fingertips,
knowing you didn't want this.
      You didn't want me.
Couldn't believe that I merely craved your essence
without concealed pretenses.
Couldn't stand my standards.
Couldn't accept the clean rep I claim
or the upfront demeanor I reign in.
You liked the idea of me.
I loved the stories you'd bring to the table
and the unstable perspective you spoke so proudly from.
You liked the idea of me.
Desired what my sultry voice would
sound like under a blue light

and seductive tension.
Let me mention that I accepted
every part of you that you disclosed.
Never dared to compose a way to change you.
Because I loved you.
But you liked the idea of me.

2 Lovers, 2 Uncompromised Lifestyles

The lifestyles of two lovers clashing,
is more treacherous than 120 shots
from a semi-automatic.
It's tragic.
All the twinkling of the eyes
and
hushed cries, are covered with unwanted tension
and much needed distance.
"I still wanna stay in this."
A thought glued to their minds but
never leaves their lips.
The tip of their hearts is cracking-
aware they have to separate
in order to obtain peace.
Two lovers.
Two uncompromised lifestyles
clashing, clanging like tambourines
trying to comprehend what the other means.
"I know this is how you get down, but what about us?"
Rushed hugs and slow gazes.
Soft kisses and wet eyes.
Two lovers with uncompromised lives,
must thrive through life without holding each other's
hearts anymore.
They'll adore each other from a distance
and reminisce the moment they were one.

Ms. Deceit

At the switch of her hips,
they came running to her side.
She blew kisses with her french tips,
inviting them for "the ride."
Her affection-glazed-deceit made them smile,
while she stole their emotions
and changed their whole lifestyle.
She became their daily devotion.
They needed her venomous embrace
and her sweet nothings whispered in their ear.
They would never give her space,
because losing her is their biggest fear.
She was no good and they knew it.
      They didn't care, "love is too hard, so screw it!"

Side-Chick

I played with the fire.
Mama told me not to.
Now,
I'm sitting in this tunnel of corpse filled memories.
Grief is breathing beneath my tears, because my fear of letting him
go has become an unbearable reality.
Painted on kisses to hide the truth of the clear canvas that I
couldn't have this man.
Painted on kisses believing that someday I may become the Mrs.
One of my many unfulfilled wishes.
I boldly blacked out the truth
of his impediment.
She was the impediment.
Moments we had under the stars are now destined to scar my
reputation,
but the sweet temptation was too sweet; I had swallow.
I'm reminiscing the hallow savor.
Every touch went deeper than the blood in my veins; I was chained
to his vibe.
His flow kept me on my toes, always leaving me on a habitual high.
I was addicted to the fire and destruction.
I played with the fire now my spirit is calloused.
Cried out for someone to open up and understand that this man

has become a part of me.
He seeped within my veins and his shadow lived behind my lust and
infatuation.
His voice was sweet to my tongue and called out to my inner being.
I thought I was seeing immanence in him.
Blindly embracing my sin.
Don't know if I should call it temptation,
It was more like anticipation-
bound to happen.
Friends asked where his girl was
my essence whispered to me "*I am she*".
Please understand that I and this man had more than just a "sensual
phase."
We were one-
or so I deliberated.
So, caught within the trap I couldn't snap out of his delicious fallacy
that he loved me.
Call me the side chick with no class.
But, please believe me; I thought he was my remedy.
I ignored the hate or obvious signs.
Disregarded the warnings and malice.
I was sure we were fate.
Since I played with fire,
currently I'm burning in the flames.
I just received this text -
his girl just got his last name.

Love

Love doesn't exclusively reside in our inner thighs.
It refuses to disrespect and it protects.
Nor does it direct one's path to deceit.
It's enticing, cupping one's flaws like fresh water
from a southern creek.
It's sweet to the soul, yet
sour to one's guards.
Love feeds off of father time-
never becoming anxious,
but always forbearing one's flaws and
shortcomings.
Then…
encourages one to progress
and profess one's true self to the world,
with no apologies.
Love doesn't only comfort.
Love embraces.
It frees and it showers peace,
even in the darkest corner of an attic.
Love isn't frantic.
It doesn't panic at the sight of trouble
or become dismayed.
It isn't swayed by storms.
Love is solid and anchored on truth.
Love is in it for the long haul.
Love does not contain envy.
There's no need for it to

sashay with a peacock strut.
Love erupts with joy, peace,
challenge, perseverance,
strength and longevity without any effort.
Love oozes 1Corinthians 13:4-7.
Love doesn't always feel like heaven.
But, it will remain by one's side and
ride out the fiery darts that feel
like hell is within.
Love is not arrogant,
nor does it possess
a chicken chest.
Love rests on authenticity and
dominates hate with its
true colors.
Love embraces one where he/she is
and walks them through
the winter.
Teaches him/her how to live out
their spring.
Loves sings diversity.
It brings forth
change to those willing
to accept transformation.
Love doesn't reside in specific situations.
It sits wherever it is accepted
and fills up whoever is receptive to
its power.

Or, Maybe I'm Too Deep

Remember when communication was easy
and being sleazy had an age requirement?
When light-up sneakers were the rave
and saying, "Dope ain't a joke" was cool?
It was simple back then.
Simplicity lived even in the most
complex situations and communication
was the key to resolution.
Now, it seems pride is celebrated.
We use text messaging and subliminal messages on social media as a
verbal substitute.
Remember when observing a face
told you all the emotions they held
and all the hurt they couldn't tell?
Remember the times we use to
sell our drawings for 50₵ and
pretended to be sick to get out of math?
We ran away from our issues back then and it seems
We still are.
But,
we take it too far now a days.
If only things were simple like it used to be.
and we were more transparent like we should be.

Cheap Shots

Cheap shots lost in translation
have become compliments.
The name, B!#℃h
can leave lips
without hesitation.
Candy coated videos covering arrogance and sensuality.
Children have become the causalities to it all.
Confused by malicious slurs,
the kiddies concur with what the media portrays.
Poor things…
Persuaded to behave and blindly become puppets
to society and its ways.
Shame.
Cheap shots lost in translation and deathly eyes that cut through soft
eyes.
Killing has become the easily
prized and crowned
"The realest, the illest of them."
Little do they know they'll die by their lifestyle like
the rest of them.
Cheap shots glamorized
and optimism ostracized, fallen in the weak category.
Positive responses are just as real as allegories.

Madness
Fraudulent jesters, parading
their foul burdens of classless humor,
into the petty prisons some of us are stuck in.
Their stench fills our nostrils,
as social media cackles at their
malicious slurs and derogatory antics.
They take their disrespect to the bank,
cashing out on another beings humiliation.
Racial attacks have always been a recycled sensation.
A form of entertainment.
Belittling always soothes the arrogant and insecure.
Integrity and empowerment is now a bore.
Disrespect, maliciousness and deceit
are now adored.

Gimme A Song

Gimme a song where it sounds like a lullaby
somebody mama sang a long time ago.
Where the lyrics are full of possibilities, high and low.
Bring back the time when love was a real thing and not just a show.
Gimme a heart that's hard as nails so when my emotions are dragged,
its trail leaves metal sparks that spark back up strength to brush off
the animosity.
Am I wrong to want this?
Probably.
But you see, the faux society we live in today, preys on the genuine
and praises
the plastic and easy.
Sleazy is the new classy, with stiletto heels and speaking words of
malevolence,
is now "keeping it real."
The seal of *making it in this world,* is to uncurl your loved ones and
break down their insides
till they bow down to you.
Because remember:
in this Faux society,
"It's all about you, so do you."
Translation:
"If it ain't about me, screw YOU."
The true soldiers of this thing throw grenades into the sea of truth
and
 hide in the trenches of rotted dreams.
Waiting for the truth to scream.

Gimme a song where it sounds like a lullaby,
somebody mama sang a long time ago, when the world was full of
possibilities high and low.
When love was a real thing and not just a show.
Gimme a heart that is hard as nails, so when my emotions are
dragged, its trail leaves metal sparks that spark back up strength to
brush off the animosity.
Possibly a lollipop too.
Sweet enough to sugar coat the lies, but kick the back of my mouth
with the truth.

The 21st Century Never Looked So Eerie

We always dreamed of unpacking
fear, paranoia, and malevolence from our hearts.
Our giants used to be
boisterous, bold and belligerent back in the day.
They'd say their hateful dreams to us so freely,
with such glee dancing, on their tongues.
They're more subtle and sophisticated now.
They've snatched our crowns while we were
busy kissing their golden painted feet.
Using our own to falsely define and inspire
us to strip off our royalty like peasant rags.
We brag over our material things while leaving
our star dust with the dogs.
The 21st century never looked this eerie.

Kings and Queens screamed from the top of their lungs
while their dignity hung from vintage trees.
They used to be stung by the men in white hoods
with raging fire and fierce voices.

My Quintessence

Now media's bees and journalism's definition of "tranquility"
leave the stinger in our skin.
We're too blind to see the subtle hate.
So distracted, we hurt our own kind
and strip off each other's identity.
The 21ˢᵗ century never looked so eerie.

We ignore our forefather's theories and bury
the truth like dead homicidal men
and pretend "It's not that serious".
It was always that serious.

We are defending deceit and burying our truth for them now.
We'd rather feed what they give us than to chase after our crowns.

Nigga

My pen leaks streaks of unwanted truth.
That your "redefinition" is artificial.
That Nigga and Nigger are still
derogatory 'til this day.
But, you're too blind to see it, too lost to
probably receive this.
So lost in phony bliss, you can't see beyond the mist.
Can't even read between the lines, you're even defiant
to learn your royal history, because you've been
blinded since your youth.
I mean, who wants to be politically correct these days anyway?
Directors and producers place glaze on our identities, so
that Nigga is an okay word to say.
It's even okay for other races to use today.
No harm, because the definition has changed.
Are you insane?
How can a term be changed
that's attached to generations of
men and women chained by their ankles
and shackled in their mind?
How can a name be redefined,
when it was designed to name the
"black monkeys" and tame "ignorant bodies",
to live in back-breaking-intellectual-lacking-folly?
How can that term be changed,
when the original beings called, Niggas are still running
through our veins?

We possess their features, yet exclaim our self-degradation
like soap box preachers.
Their struggles and pain run through our veins.
We have the eyes of our great aunties and uncles.
We often leave their stories on library shelves,
along with their thoughts on dignity.
Even though we have their lips, their hair, their strength
and bold glares that stare off into the distance.
Their battles are now our victories, but
we still have battles of our own.
But silicone is the current subject
and disrespecting our own kind is
more normal than positive unity.
"Oh, we have bigger fish to fry"
Then wonder why we can't get anywhere.
One cannot move forward without acknowledging
one's history and understanding one's identity.
Nigga is not an original identification
and there's no justification for such folly
to answer to such trash.
Excuse my brash tone.
It's still the same term.
You all have been conned.
Your minds have been fondled.
So busy poppin' molly,
you probably left your crown on
your night stand.
Please understand, we have enough
outsiders spewing out verbal darts.
We don't need to ride on our own kind too.

"Jazzy, It's Not That Serious"

We're real quick to slit the necks of our own kind instead of finding a resolution without bussin' a 9.
We're back in the 60's, we need a revolution.
Gave into visual prostitution and affirmation is our wage.
Engaged by violence that feeds our egos.
Hedonistic leeches have become our heroes.
It's *funny*.
We lift up the mummies who love *hoes, drugs and money*
and crucify the remnant for challenging such folly.
Probably so lost in our selfish gain, we can't see that they're getting a big percentage of what we gain.
It's insane how we sing songs of hatred, disgusted with what's sacred, describe material wealth as greatness and integrity overrated.
We teach our kids indirect malevolence and expect character to be prevalent.
Then, leave the teachers to blame and cover the shame of our botched home training.
"Jazzy, it's not that serious."
Are you delirious?
No one is anybody's keeper, which is why unity is a dead name.
Which is why the oppressor can call us deranged when we dare fight for change.
Which is why they don't need to *arrange* intimidation cause we as a people are already estranged.
It is that serious.
We exchanged Sisterhood and Brotherhood for

packaged goods
and narcissistic slogans that leave us more broken than a shattered
chandelier.
Beautifully intricate pieces that can only be repaired with unity.
We are a community that's slowly dying from outside oppressors
and...
by
our
own
hands.
We can ban the outside abuse, but what about our own hands?
We brand our stereotypes like fads and get mad when the outsiders
find it entertaining to demean us with our *personal jokes*.
They poke fun at the folks that damn near build their foundations
for generations but we're too busy walking proudly
with our self-degradation.
It is that serious.
I'm curious to know when you'll ever find it to be serious.
Many have already died from peer to peer crime.
Are you waiting for your crew to be on that line?
Millions have experienced injustice is it okay as long
as your fine?
When one individual is hurt, so are you.
Cause it could have been you.
It is that serious.
We must stop walking over lumps in our carpet
and lift it up to address our problem.

Too many stigmas, I'm tired of looking way up the top
from the very bottom.
It is that serious.

Do You Hear the Thunder?

We sweet talk our guns and abandon the butter.
I often wonder if we hear the thunder from those
who came before.
Have we heard the rumbles, rolls and roars?
Seen the lighting flashing reminding us,
the emperor hasn't changed his clothes?
He doesn't need to.
Shoot, the wardrobe is now see- through
and we *still* can't see the truth.
Still reject the light since it doesn't
shine like our glittered lashes,
doesn't shade our insecurities
like make-up and sunglasses.
No.
It illuminates the empty voids,
reveals our nakedness and admires
our scars.
It annihilates the bars and reminds us
who's really in charge.
Yes, it bombards our ignorance of our
own identities and soothes us into the
reality of our priceless worth.
The truth hurts-
but only for a moment.
It strips us of our botched self-worth
and returns our crowns to us.
But, some of us are too blind to get down
that way.
Too swayed by the touch of
overly valued possessions.

Content that our beauty is sold on concession stands.
Unsighted that we demand to be disrespected and
become confused when our children
are defected, de-valued, lost and snatched
by the waves of death-
No.
The emperor doesn't need to change
his clothes; we're already calling ourselves
niggas and hoes.
This is what we chose.
But, it's not what we're meant to be.
Please open your mind,
come and see
that our identities are not based on what we
see on TV.
Not founded on the neighborhood we reside in
or the little cubicle we hide in.
Look within and follow your history.
Then, move forward and chase the mysteries.
Be okay with not knowing it all.
Be okay with being broken with your crown.
Chase the dreams they told you, you couldn't catch.
Light the match and cause empowering flames.
Cause change when they said you were nothing.
Be yourself, because your lilol' purpose maybe
the start of something.

Walls of Jericho

There is a battle underneath my chest.
The beating of war drums synchronized
with my heart beats and it never misses a pulse,
never loses focus to the tempo of hope.
Constant hands beating on the hollow
oak that sirens aggressive transitions.
No remission of sound, no signs of
losing momentum as I walk around my Jericho,
as I scream at our Jericho.

I will no longer be silent.
No longer place the tape over
my mouth for my oppressors.
I have chosen to become a transgressor
to hate and shame.
I have decided to march around my Jericho,
scream at our walls of malicious echoes
unjust scenarios, manipulative stereos that
exudes manipulation.
My words, my actions, my heart will bellow
until the walls of our Jericho crumble at our feet.
Until the discreet voices,
once trampled underneath fear and confusion,
remember their lives are more imperative
than the dismantled image they were given
for themselves.

There is a battle underneath my chest,
Pre-meditated tambourines playing
for the future victory.
Cymbals could never sound so good

underneath this chest of mine.
I will no longer define my identity by
the poisonous snakes in Eden.
Or the Pharisees with blind, lofty eyes.
I will no longer disguise the melody of
my sashaying soul.
I will tell my stories around our Jericho.
Unashamedly love my core until
I adore it.

There is a battle underneath my chest.
The beating of war drums synchronized
with my heart beats and it never misses a pulse,
never loses focus to the tempo of hope.
Constant hands beating on the hollow
oak that sirens aggressive transition.
No remission of sound, no signs of
losing momentum as I walk around my Jericho
as I scream at our Jericho.

I will no longer be silent.
We will be victorious with our various
colors of love, diverse melodies and sound.
We will shake the ground with the profound
stories our feet tell around the walls of
our Jericho.
It will be crumbled and the oppressors will
suffer from guilt, humility and vertigo.
There is a battle underneath my chest.
The beating of war drums synchronized
with my heart beats and it never misses a pulse,
never loses focus to the tempo of hope.

Unity

     A word.
An inanimate term that's used to
eradicate injustice, expose sinister actions and place
genocide under the telescope for the masses
to challenge.
A vintage delivery
that left timeless effects, overdrawn victories, and unanimous respect
but...
sometimes iniquitous genocide.

Unity.
     A long-lost motion
of quiet intimidation,
insufficient hesitation and
oneness that released no limitations.

Unity,
     We miss you.
you snatched fear from its pedestal
made people kill their cruel intentions
and hidden agendas, in order to conquer
uncivil practices, social murderers and lost children.

Unity,
     you're a lost song that we need
to listen to on repeat, until love comes from
the discreet place of our mind and recycles itself into others.
Your lyrics profess
change,
wisdom,
revolution,
and that everybody is everybody's keeper.
No one is left behind.

Unity,
        We need you.
A nation destitute of
accountability,
integrity,
and
peace.
Darn it, we need you to teach
my generation
some manners and
soothe our wounds with love until
our glorified anger ceases.
Until the knowledge of our purpose increases.

Unity,
        I'll welcome you.
Even if only three people open their arms too.

About the Introduction: A Note to You, The Reader

This book is a big chunk of my quintessence. From seasons I have endured, to what I stand for and wish to see in this society. However, I wanted the reader to get a feel of who I am in a nutshell. I wanted to write a poem that explained me all together without writing a scroll. Well, gosh darn it, I did it!

I was born in Manhattan, New York, in a neighborhood called *the village* at Saint Vincent's hospital. Sadly, it has since closed down in recent years. I still hang around the village and my best friend got me hooked to this one vegetarian restaurant called, *Saki*. I am not a vegetarian.

Introduction shows my silly side, as well as my stern side and my new confidence. 2014 was a tough year for me; however, oddly enough in the midst of my struggles and mishaps, I embraced all of me. I gained a confidence that I thought I would never obtain unless I smoked the brain of super hero. I digress. I am an owner of unicorns and they're all fearless divas. Their manes are nicely combed with cocoa butter smooth brushes and their horns don't reek of obnoxious vibes. *The Introduction*, oozes with self-acceptance and love for my own style of poetry. I love internal rhyming and it falls out of my mind with no shame. I am a lover of personification and similes. I cannot withhold my love for alliteration.

"I'm awesomely awkward and
ridiculously random..."

I am not quiet, but I am quite shy and observant before I share my voice with the lovely people in this world. I am a part of the over thinking club and I recently learned that the club is over populated. I was belittled or frowned upon whenever I was "too sensitive". I learned that that's how I am made and we can't have a world filled with caste iron hearts. We need some mushy folk to help others heal, move forward and be in tune with other people's responses. Besides, us sensitive folk make the best of friends. On the other hand, I am guarded and give faux smiles occasionally. Defensive and straight forward, I am human like most of my readers.

"Fragile like white lilies, but I'm firm;
I'm stern when I need to be.
Rarely butter up my words or look for honey."

Although, simply embracing myself completely doesn't mean the journey is over. I am a firm believer in changing one's self for the better, because being receptive to growth is imperative. In addition, I am always willing to adjust old habits that delay my walk towards finding myself. My lifelong goal, is to be the best me I can be.

"Far from coy when stating my boundaries.
I can be transparent like a diary
and guarded like Sloman Shields.
But, I always yield to growth."

I am a Christian. Yes, Lovely, I don't believe this world was created without a creator. I believe we are all made on this earth for a purpose. All of us strutting around with our unique personalities and styles, is not a coincidence. I know God inscribed my purpose before I was even a thought in my parents' minds. I am still learning what that is, while living confidently in what I know so far. What saddens me these days is that respecting each other, no matter our different beliefs and cultures, is a vintage idea.

"I'm Queen of the kinks.
I used to be a part of the voiceless tribe,
until God inscribed me with purpose. I no longer feel worthless;
no longer a believer in my own pessimism."

I hope you were able to relate to *My Quintessence,* while feeling challenged and encouraged; in addition to chuckling a bit!